BODY OF LIFE

BODY *of* LIFE

Elizabeth Alexander

TIA CHUCHA PRESS
LOS ANGELES

ACKNOWLEDGMENTS

These poems first apeared in the following publications:

Ploughshares ("Harlem Birthday Party")
Word ("Tending," "Summertime")
Crab Orchard Review ("Body of Life")
Voice Literary Supplement ("Affirmative Action Blues," "Float")
Chicago Review ("Frank Willis," "Alka-Seltzer," "Blues")
Poetry ("Cough Medicine," "Apollo," "Equinox," "Manhattan Elegy,"
    "L.A. By Night," "Stravinsky in L.A.," "At the Beach")
The Kenyon Review ("Diva Studies," "Dream," "Haircut," "In the Small Rooms"
The William and Mary Review ("Cleaning out Your Apartment," "Aspirin," "Fugue"
Callaloo ("Butter," "Passage," "What I'm Telling You," "Family Stone")
The Paris Review ("Dream #3," "After")
The Indiana Review ("Compass," "The Texas Prophet")
Yellow Silk ("Sonnet")

Grateful acknowledgment is made to the editors of these journals. The author would also like to thank the Corporation of Yaddo, the Ragdale Foundation, The National Endowment for the Arts, and the University of Chicago's Chicago Humanities Institute, as well as the friends, fellow poets, and family members who encouraged the writing of these poems.

Printed in the United States. Reprinted in 2009.

ISBN 13-978-1-882688-12-8

Library of Congress Catalogue Card Number: 96-61081

Book Design: Jane Brunette
Cover painting: Kerry James Marshall, "Could This Be Love," 1992, 84" x 96"

PUBLISHED BY:

Tia Chucha Press
A project of Tia Chucha's Centro Cultural
PO Box 328
San Fernando, CA 91341
www.tiachucha.com

DISTRIBUTED BY:

Northwestern University Press
Chicago Distribution Center
11030 South Langley Avenue
Chicago IL 60628

Tia Chucha Press is the publishing wing of Tia Chucha's Centro Cultural, Inc., a 501(c)3 nonprofit corporation. Tia Chucha's Centro Cultural has received funding from the National Endowment for the Arts, the California Arts Council, Los Angeles County Arts Commission, Los Angeles Department of Cultural Affairs, The California Community Foundation, the Annenberg Foundation, Thrill Hill Foundation, the Middleton Foundation, Not Just Us Foundation, among others, as well as donations from Bruce Springsteen, John Densmore, Lou Adler, Richard Foos, Adrienne Rich, Tom Hayden, Dave Marsh, Mel Gilman, Jack Kornfield, Jesus Trevino, David Sandoval, Denise Chávez and John Randall of the Border Book Festival, Luis & Trini Rodríguez, and more.

Table of Contents

I.

II.

III.

IV.

Then I imagine life would flood
my whole being
better still I would feel it
touching me or biting me
lying down I would see
the finally free odors come to me
like merciful hands
finding their way
to sway their long hair in me
longer than this past that I cannot reach.

Aimé Césaire
"Lost Body"

PART I

Stravinsky in L.A.

In white pleated trousers, peering through green
sunshades, looking for the way the sun is red
noise, how locusts hiss to replicate the sun.
What is the visual equivalent
of syncopation? Rows of seared palms wrinkle
in the heat waves through green glass. Sprinklers
tick, tick, tick. The Watts Towers aim to split
the sky into chroma, spires tiled with rubble
nothing less than aspiration. I've left
minarets for sun and syncopation,
sixty-seven shades of green which I have
counted, beginning: palm leaves, front and back,
luncheon pickle, bottle glass, etcetera.
One day I will comprehend the different
grades of red. On that day I will comprehend
these people, rhythms, jazz, Simon Rodia,
Watts, Los Angeles, aspiration.

The Josephine Baker Museum

1. East St. Louis (1918)

Mama danced
a glass
of water balanced
on her head.

"Someone raped
a white woman!
We ran
at night,
next day
heard tell

of eyes
plucked out,
of scalps
pulled clean,
a bloody sky.

That day
God showed
his face,
grey and shaggy,
in the rain clouds.

2. Costumes

The black and white checked overalls
I wore off the boat at Le Havre. Wired skirts
whose trains weigh fifty pounds. Furling,
curling headpieces, and hourglass-
shaped gowns.

Schiparellis and Poirets! The green suede
Pilgrim shoes and orange jacket,
Harlem-made. The lime chiffon!
the one with egrets
painted on.

I'm sick of *touts le bananes.* Ici,
my uniform: French Air Force, fray-spots
blackened back with ink. And here,
the diamond necklace,
for my glorious Chiquita.

3. The Wig Room

A gleaming black sputnik of hair.
A solid figure-eight of hair, glazed black.
Crows' wings of hair, a waist-length switch.

Black profiteroles of mounded hair.
Hair like a Eiffel Tower, painted black.
A ziggurat of patent leather hair.

Black crowns to be taken on and off, that live
in the room when the lights go out, a roomful
of whispering Josephines, a roomful
of wigs in the dark.

4. *Ablutions*

In the cinema Mammy hands Scarlett
white underthings to cover her white skin.
I am both of them and neither, tall,
tan, terrific, soaking in my tub of milk.

What would it mean to be me on stage
in a bathtub soaping, singing my French
chansons with one pointed foot with painted toes
suggesting what is underneath, suggesting

dusky, houri dreams and is she really
naked? Do they really want to see
the nappy pussy underneath that sweats
and stinks and grinds beneath bananas,

turns to seaweed in the tub? What if
I let my hair go back, or dressed
more often as a man? What if I let myself
get fat? What would it mean to step out

of the bathtub onto the stage and touch
myself, do to myself what I do to myself
in the bedroom when only my animals
watch? What would I be to my audience then?

(Sigh) Come here, baby. Dry me off.

5. *Diva Studies*

What is original, what
is facsimile? The boys
in the dressing room are showing
me how to skin my hair down flat
like patent leather, black as that.
I show them how to paint eyeballs
on their eyelids to look bright
from the last row, how I line
my eyes like the Egyptian cat.
We carry on, in that dingy,
musky, dusty room overhung
with fraying costumes, peeling
sequins, shedding feathers, mules
with broken heels, mending glue, eye-
lash glue, charcoal sticks and matches,
brushes and unguents and bottles of oil.
The dressing room is my schoolhouse.
My teachers are men more woman
than actual women, and I
am the skinny sixteen-year old
whose hair is slicked flat because
Congoleum burned it off.
I cross my eyes and knock my knees,
am somehow still a diva.
The boys swoop past and are rare.
The beauty is how this strange
trade works. The truth of it is,
we are fabulous.

Yolande Speaks

*Yolande Du Bois was the only
daughter of W.E.B. Du Bois*

I know some call him
"Doctor Dubious."

I hear how people
talk. I know who's

called my marriage
counterfeit. I know

who thinks me stupid.
I would love

the peace and quiet
of stupidity,

having witnessed
the hot hiss of

true intelligence,
a white noise, a

camphor that over-
takes the globe.

I have laughed
at my father's gloves

and spats. My pace
is my own. I am

a sputtering
cadmium light

turning on
like the R.K.O.

Radio Tower.

Fugue

Virginia Woolf, incested
through her childhood, wrote
that she imagined herself
growing up inside a grape.
Grapes are sealed and safe.
You wouldn't quite float
in one; you'd sit locked
in enough moisture to keep
from drying out, the world
outside through gelid green.
Picture everyone's edges
smudged. Picture everyone
a green as delicate
as a Ming celadon. Pic-
ture yourself a mollusk
with an unsegmented body
in a skin so tight and taut
that you'd be safe. You could
ruminate all night about
the difference between "taut"
and "tight," "molest" and "incest."
"Taut" means tightly-drawn,
high-strung. What is tight
is structured so as not to
permit passage of liquid
or gas, air, or light.

The Texas Prophet

I am the Texas Prophet who is now in Baltimore.
God blesses those that see me and I'm coming to your town.
I guarantee you without fail a straight and one-way blessing.
I come to bring you luck and by your popular demand.

I'm bringing Mojo hands for those of you can't win for losing.
All manner of disease is healed. Cash money falls like rain.
If I were you I would come early. He can't stay all night.
Those who know me know I am no money-hungry Prophet.

I am the Texas Prophet who is now in Baltimore.
I'm bringing good luck talismans and guarantee my work.
Keep looking up keep looking up His help is on the way.
Yours in spirit and in love The Prophet John C. Bates.

Minnesota Fats Describes His Youth

I've been eating
like a sultan
since I was two days old.

I had a mother
and three sisters
who worshipped me.

When I was two years old
they used to plop me
in a bed with a jillion

satin pillows
and spray me
with exotic perfumes

and lilac water,
and then
they would shoot me the grapes.

Talk Radio, D.C.

Leave fatback and a copper penny
on a wound 'til it draw out the poison,
'til the penny turn green.

Tobacco's what works on a bee-sting,
but for poison ivy – I'm serious, now –
catch your first morning urine in your hands
and splash it on that rash.

When they had the diptheria epidemic
I was burning up with fever, burning and burning.
When the doctor left the house, my grandmother
snuck in the back door with a croaker sack of mackerel.
She wrapped me all up in that salt mackerel.
The next morning, my fever had broke
and the fish was all cooked.

Passage

Henry Porter wore good clothes for his journey,
the best his wife could make from leftover
cambric, shoes stolen from the master. They
bit his feet, but if he took them off he feared
he'd never get them on again. He needed
to look like a free man when he got there.
Still in a box in the jostling heat,
nostrils to a board pried into a vent,
(a peephole, too, he'd hoped, but there was only
black to see) there was nothing to do
but sleep and dream and weep. Sometimes the dreams
were frantic, frantic loneliness an acid
at his heart. Freedom was near but un-
imaginable. Anxiety roiled inside
of him, a brew which corroded his stomach,
whose fumes clamped his lungs and his throat.
When the salt-pork and cornbread were finished
he dreamed of cream and eggs but the dreams
made him sick. He soiled himself and each time
was ashamed. He invented games, tried to
remember everything his mother
ever told him, every word he hadn't
understood, every vegetable he'd ever
eaten (which was easy: kale, okra, corn,
carrots, beans, chard, yams, dandelion greens),
remember everyone's name who had ever
been taken away. The journey went that way.

When he got there, his suit was chalky
with his salt, and soiled, the shoes waxy with blood.
The air smelled of a surfeit of mackerel.
Too tired to weep, too tired to look through
the peephole and see what freedom looked like,
he waited for the man to whom he'd shipped
himself: Mister William Still, Undertaker,
Philadelphia. He repeated the last
words he'd spoken to anyone: goodbye
wife Clothilde, daughter Eliza,
best friend Luke. Goodbye, everyone, goodbye.
When I can, I'll come for you. I swear,
I'll come for you.

PART II

Summertime

Where we live there are caged peacocks
in summertime, heavy in the heat,
bald-headed, dragging their tails, which,
once a season, they unfurl. Objects
wrinkle in the heat waves rising
from the pavement. A dead rat
in the back alley gets a proper
burial from a girl who can flip
her eyelids inside out, and at
the funeral I wear my white
go-go boots and sing "I Gotta Be Me."
We buy coverless comic books
cut-rate, impossibly red
vending machine pistachios
which stain our hands. A hydrant
illicitly opened, kids riding
the hard spray, caught in the rainbow
of water. On television,
Senators talk, talk talk.
A Wham-O Superball bounces
off a sidewalk crack and into
the cosmos. A red rubber planet
could bounce to the sky and stick.

Aspirin

Bayer's children's aspirin is cheaper
than St. Joseph's, I know, because
Bayer's is what we buy, so I want
St. Joseph's, the tiny peach teeth,
the chalky crumble.

           Sometimes I long
for the fevers of my childhood.
I'd turn radiant and magenta
and see cheetahs in my bedroom,
the grey rug turned to elephant
hide, damp sheets, mosquito net –

I miss actual delirium,
the hot brain burning through its caul
to imagination.

Cough Medicine

Grape Robitussen tastes like melted lollipop.
It sits by my bed, heroin melting in a spoon.
I want it. I want the grape. I want to sleep.

Already in school they have had us read books
where the junkie goes cold turkey, shakes and shivers
on a cot. I am an opium-eater

who swigs from the bottle, falls into swollen sleep.
I ride the HORSE. I have a MONKEY on my back.
Already I am the kind of child who should not

be allowed to read so much or late at night.
But now I am coughing like the consumptives
in my books, match-girls black from chimney dust,

and if I cough I cannot sleep; if I don't sleep
I cannot dream of all I'm reading: bony fingers
that snap off and turn to candy, children who slip

down the bathtub drain, who are frozen in place forever.

Bossa Nova

The color green
which is the backdrop
for the whipped cream-

covered woman
on the jacket
of Brasil '66,

Herb Alpert and
the Tijuana Brass.
The woman puts one

whipped-cream finger
to her tongue,
which is red and I

imagine prickly. It
is nineteen-sixty-six
and this is Sexy.

Remember those hips-
ter horns, Brasil
for beginners, Oh!

I was born during
the bossa nova craze.
In nineteen sixty-six

I was four years old
and this was the record
that made me dance.

Washington Etude

After rain, mushrooms
appear in the park
but you can not eat them.

1967,
the year of the locust.
They come to Northwest

Washington by millions
and for days I crunch
shed husks beneath my feet

as they rattle and hiss
their rage from the trees.
Baby teeth bite baby

onion grass and honey-
suckle nipples, tiny
tongue balancing

the clear, sweet drops.
I am a humming-
bird, a cat who laps

cream from a bowl.
Dandelions
are yellow one day,

white the next. A mud-

puddle surrounded
by brambles and black-

berries is where God lives.
Buttercups under
my chin tell me all

I need to know. Nothing
blue occurs naturally
in Washington, someone

says, and I believe it.
I'm put to bed
when it's still light

and hear other children
playing out my window,
watch daylight bow,

regard the flare
of blooming stars,
the cicada's maraca.

Apollo

We pull off
to a road shack
in Massachusetts
to watch men walk

on the moon. We did
the same thing
for three two one
blast off, and now

we watch the same men
bounce in and out
of craters. I want
a Coke and a hamburger.

Because the men
are walking on the moon
which is now irrefutably
not green, not cheese,

not a shiny dime floating
in a cold blue,
the way I'd thought,
the road shack people don't

notice we are a black
family not from there,
the way it mostly goes.
This talking through

static, bouncing in space-
boots, tethered
to cords is much
stranger, stranger

even than we are.

What I'm Telling You

If I say, my father was Betty Shabazz's lawyer, the poem can
go no further. I've given you the punchline. If you know
who she is, all you can think about is how and what you
want to know about me, about my father, about Malcolm,
especially in 1990 when he's all over t-shirts and medallions,
but what I'm telling you is that Mrs. Shabazz was a nice
lady to me, and I loved her name for the wrong reasons,
SHABAZZ! and what I remember is going to visit her
daughters in 1970 in a dark house with little furniture and
leaving with a candy necklace the daughters gave me, to
keep. Now that children see his name and call him, Malcolm
Ten, and someone called her Mrs. Ex-es, and they don't
really remember who he was or what he said or how he
smiled the way it happened when it did, and neither do I,
I think about how history is made more than what happened
and about a nice woman in a dark house filled with
daughters and candy, something dim and unspoken,
expectation.

Butter

My mother loves butter more than I do,
more than anyone. She pulls chunks off
the stick and eats it plain, explaining
cream spun around into butter! Growing up
we ate turkey cutlets sauteed in lemon
and butter, butter and cheese on green noodles,
butter melting in small pools in the hearts
of Yorkshire puddings, butter better
than gravy staining white rice yellow,
butter glazing corn in slipping squares,
butter the lava in white volcanoes
of hominy grits, butter softening
in a white bowl to be creamed with white
sugar, butter disappearing into
whipped sweet potatoes, with pineapple,
butter melted and curdy to pour
over pancakes, butter licked off the plate
with warm Alaga syrup. When I picture
the good old days I am grinning greasy
with my brother, having watched the tiger
chase his tail and turn to butter. We are
Mumbo and Jumbo's children despite
historical revision, despite
our parent's efforts, glowing from the inside
out, one hundred megawatts of butter.

Compass

I.

I swing
the thin tin
arm to mark
an arc
from pole
to pole: my
mother's compass
spans the world.
It marks
the globe from east
to west on this
white paper as
I twirl
the compass,
hear the hush
of graphite:
a horizon.

II.

It feels freest
at its widest set,
held just by a pin-
prick on the page,
moored and precarious,
like Mathew Henson's flag.

III.

Even the dogs died.
His Eskimo grandchildren cried

when, years later, the black man
they prayed was a Henson

came looking to figure
what makes a man hazard

ten lifetimes of snow. Hayden
imagined your arguments, hunger,

delirium. The fur of your hood
frames your brown face like petals or rays.

To stand where the top of the world curves.
To look all around in that silence.

To breathe in cold air that has never
been squandered, breathe out again.

To breathe in cold air, to breathe
in . . . out . . .

breathe in

Alka-Seltzer

My mother lets me
have it every night,

I tell the 'sitter,
who comes Saturdays,

ignores us for Motown,
my mother's high heels.

She's diabetic,
Mother whispers, please

Behave.
       When the baby-

sitter thinks we are
sleeping she peeps

through the door-crack
and giggles. I see

her eyes and never
sleep, not ever.

She locks the bathroom
door, to take her

medicine, she says.
We bang when she's been gone

too long. "I'm cleaning
out my bunny-hole,"

she says, "with witch-
hazel."

    She sees me
read the dictionary,

asks me words. Do you
know what this is?

Say it. Do you know
this other word?

Say it. Do you know
what a pussy is?

A cat, I say. Then
say it. The word

in my mouth like gristle
or giblets, a stone

in the rice, by mistake.
I run upstairs and

later pee the bed,
and later curse

the babysitter dead. Next
time she comes I say

I have a disease
in my stomach, I need

Alka-Seltzer, like
insulin, in cold

water, in my favorite
glass, the one etched

with turquoise horsemen,
the taste on my tongue

of metal, salt, and lemons.

Frank Willis

I am in the four percent
of adults 18-29 who told
George Gallup they know
"a lot" about Watergate.
"Watergate" was the building
near the Howard Johnson's where
we'd go when school let out for summer
and eat clam strips. Water-
gate was where we stopped
in carpool one year to fetch
the sickly boy for day camp,
where I danced in toe shoes
to the Beach Boys, in shame.
Growing up in Washington
I rode D.C. Transit, knew Senators,
believed the Washington Monument
was God's pencil because my friend
Jennifer said so, never went
to the Jefferson Memorial,
climbed the stone rhino
at the Smithsonian, cursed tourists,
took exquisite phone messages
for my father, a race man,
who worked for the government –
I held his scrawled hate mail to the light.

I don't care now that Chuck Colson
has a prison ministry, or that G.
Gordon Liddy ate a rat.

The summer I was eleven Water-
gate was something I watched
with my grandmother on TV like the best
soap opera but also like something
she would have called "civic," the things
you had to know. Today in some way
I somehow care that Frank Willis lives
with his mother, without employ,
was arrested for stealing
a $12 pair of sneakers, told Jet
it was "a total mix-up," somehow know
there is meaning in Jet's tending the fate
of this man who saw the tape
on the office door latch. Cog, cog,
cog in the wheel of history, Frank
Willis in Jet these years later,
like the shouted spray-paint on an empty
garage in my parent's back alley:
"Aaron Canaday," his name alone
enough, and then a sentence,
a song: "Slick was Here-O."

Family Stone

We drive "The Nutmeg State" in summer.
Daddy sings "Your Feets Too Big." You lie!
we scream, there's no such song. You lie! we scream, at
"Buttermilk Sky." We beg for more,
then beg for WAVZ-13. The O'Jays sing
"Backstabbers," then Sly Stone.

                    We believe
it's a family affair, believe in someone
named Sly, something called a family stone because
it's on the radio today –

   and so on
   and so on
   and scooby dooby dooby

– but this other language, Daddy singing
"your pedal extremities are collosal,"
and who ever tasted buttermilk, and why
is he called "Hoagy," is something else

all together. These old-heads who are
my parents come from New York City,
from another tribe. We are the DeeCee kids
and think we don't speak jazz. But we will dream
that night, after wide eyes to stars sharp
as the word "Connecticut," dream of mammoth
feet with painted toes, buckets of clabber, sirens.

Manhattan Elegy

I left behind a mother, father,
baby brother, town-house, door bell, family-
sized gallons of two-percent milk, for
my grandmother's apartment near
the United Nations, her apartment
building with elevator, incinerator
chute, intercom with buzzer,
deliveries from Gristede's. There I had
a godfather who took me out to lunch,
great-aunts who took me to tea,
a great-uncle who took me to the Museum
of the City of New York, and a grand-
father who took me on the IRT.
I was the only child in all Manhattan.

My grandmother loved the Museum
of Modern Art, Matisse's revelers,
the red parlor with goldfish. She loved
the rough-cut oil of "Starry Night" and Monet's
lily ponds, took me after to a hotel
dining room just like "Hello, Dolly!"
where the violinist asked for my song,
and I didn't have one, and how, she said,
could an eight-year old lady not know
a serenade? She took me to Broadway
and home on the cross-town bus.

The U.N. tulips reminded me of Holland,
my eight-year old idea of Holland, like
in Mary Poppins when "Canada"
was grasshoppers and roses in white snow,
a beautiful word. I watched my grandmother
summon friends to come see me from the pages
of her red kid address book: Dorothy
and Kay, Mae, Phyllis, Helena and Eddie,
Lucille, Louise. Venetian blinds, taxi-
cabs, milk by the quart, lambchops and water-
cress, brass candle snifters. Permit me
to sing this kaddish for New York,
New York, my city of adults.

My Grandmother's New York Apartment

1. Apartment

Everything pulled out or folded away:
sofa into a bed, tray tables that dis-
appear behind a door, everything
transmutable, alchemy in small
spaces, even my grandmother tiny
and changeable: a housecoat and rollers
which vanish and become an Irish
tweed suit, a tilted chapeau, a Hello
in the elevator just like, as she
would say, the Queen of Denmark.

2. Bathroom

Cuticle cream and orange sticks, bath oil pearls,
cotton wisps, boxed perfume in a lower
drawer, wire rollers, seaweedy stockings
drying on a rod, white garter belts,

white cotton gloves and Vaseline at night,
nail lacquer, tweezers, red lipsticks.
Push against your front teeth so they don't
go buck. Grease elbows, hair-ends, kneecaps, lips.

Grandmother smoked on the toilet at night.
Stop chewing your nails, stop picking your face.
Here is a diamond-dust fingernail file.
Your brand new rain-bonnet lost already?

In the Small Rooms

Under the big house, above the pool, surrounded
by flowers, to the side of the sea on a bed
in a room that I share with my brother is an X-
marks the spot that is me. I am ten years old. I have
finished the fifth grade and now know Spanish: *Usted*
está aquí. The people we are visiting
wear white every day. In the kitchen is a pantry
filled with King Oscar sardines and saltine crackers
from the mainland. In the living room my father
teaches us the stock market with a full bowl
of walnuts. We go on trips some days, my mother,
father, brother, me: to a sulfur spring that turns
earrings and belt-buckles black, on a sailboat
where we watch flying fish stitch the sea, to town
to buy duty-free Chivas for my grandfather,
my first wrist-watch (I will later stop its time
in water and tell no one), Wedgewood teacups
for my mother. Tiny lizards, quick and curved
as punctuation appear on the walls, sleep
in our shoes, flick their tongues at us and vanish.
There is a woman who cooks and a woman who cleans,
a man who tends the pool and gardens and a young man
who helps him and runs errands. This young man appears
in some photos from that visit, in the background.
All of them live here, in the small rooms beneath the big
house in back where my brother and I go by mistake
and find the kittens, grey and mewling, so new
they could die without their mother. Unfortunately
I have read Black Boy, where the boy kills the kitten

whose mews disturb his father, and unfortunately,
I have told it to my brother. We cuddle the babies
and have to be summoned for dinner. We smell
a different dinner cooking in the small rooms.

For years I remember this much only: my feet
on cool marble slap-slapping through the big house, my feet
on rough gravel, my feet on hot slate stones. My room cool
and dark and square like a flower box to be planted
but no one else, anywhere. The generator humming,
the electric snap of the mosquito-zapper.
I suck on the ends of my pigtails and taste
sea-salt. Where are my favorite white sandals,
my plastic sunglasses? The young man who carries
crates of sardines, who digs weeds from the garden and
bottle glass from the beach and skims leaves and dead lizards
off of the top of the pool is lying on top
of me and for years that is all I will remember.

What am I not remembering   Why didn't I tell
How had I learned if I said what happened
he could lose his job   it would be my fault   It won't be
until different friends remember and tell me about
a father who made her speak dirty words, a mother
who laughed when she walked into a room and saw
"Uncle" down her daughter's underpants, a brother
who came into her bed for years 'til he shrank
to the size of a migraine headache and moved
inside her skull, that my picture can go further:
the dim room, it's lunchtime, I am not ten but eight.
I am grown now, old enough to want fingers
in my vagina but I don't because no matter
who there is dirt beneath their fingernails. There's dirt
in my vagina, dirt and lizards. Take them out.

PART III

Six Yellow Stanzas

1.

Didn't know what to do
at the Boule Ball,
so I put on a Mardi Gras mask
of a smile and watched
those Creoles second-line,
light yellow faces, bright
white kerchiefs waving
back and forth
made languid light.

2.

Langour.
I lay back
in the bucket seat,
for the first time
let a yellow boy
kiss me and kiss me and kiss me,
talk that talk.

3.

I don't know how
to talk that talk.
I am visiting friends
of a family friend.
These Creole ways
are something I
have never seen
before or since.
Yellow boys squire me
to glittering clubs
where I am the coal
in the Christmas stocking.
Curious, curious
yellow me. I can't
tell who among
these creamy
freesia women –
they all are.
They let some men
be dark, like the one
they call Dark Gable,
who could talk
that talk the best.
The club is dark.
Some men are dark.
The women shine
and glitter. Me.

4.

Photograph:
my yellow moon-
pie face, yellow baby
screaming in the middle of the bed.
You could pass for Spanish,
a man says, as a compliment.
You a high-yella gal, and I like that,
says a suitor. Yellow!

I dreamed I had a yellow baby.
In the dream I didn't feed it.
It dried flat on the blacktop
like an old squashed frog.
I tried to revive it with lemonade
by the dropperful,
but that was the end
of my yellow dream baby.

5.

My thigh next to your thigh.
Your black thigh
(your dark brown thigh)
next to my black thigh
(which is "yellow"
and brown, and black.)
Sunless flesh or sunshine flesh.
I startle myself
with my yellowness
next to your black
but say none of this,
and lick your skin 'til yellow-
black sparks fly,

a hive of bumblebees
which hum at your body
and do not sting.

6.

Egg yolk, crocus, buttercup, butter,
dandelion, sunflower, sunbeam, sun,
chicken fat, legal pads, bumble-bee stripes,
a bowl full of lemons, grapefruit peel,
iris hearts, pollen, the Coleman's mustard can,
the carpet and sheets in my childhood bedroom:
things that are yellow and yellow alone.

Float

It is 1978 and I am floating
on a raft in a backyard swimming pool,
having been to the Prom the night before,
having stayed out through breakfast,
having worn a red dress that is stained now
with blackberries, having kissed my face raw,
having touched, having been finger-fucked. Washington,
D.C. is hot in early June; the sun
is on my face and the Commodores
are on the radio singing "Zoom." I am jangled
with sleeplessness, amplified with lust, and lust
is a spirochete, a burrowing corkscrew of pleasure.
The Floaters sing "Float, Float On,"
which is how I am drifting on this raft,
metabolizing my father's rage, which erupts
in Morse code burps: Empty
the garbage, Sweep the deck, Dot Dot Dit,
anything but what he is upset about.
I have been bad.

I love how lust quickens and quickens, not stopping,
the pace, the pitch, my clitoris a clock in fast motion,
hands spinning madly on an axis. I love how paper
pages tear away from calendars in the movies, love
that I can remember everything. I am spinning
like that all the time now, or else I am perfectly still.

Blues

I am lazy, the laziest
girl in the world. I sleep during
the day when I want to, 'til
my face is creased and swollen,
'til my lips are dry and hot. I
eat as I please: cookies and milk
after lunch, butter and sour cream
on my baked potato, foods that
slothful people eat, that turn
yellow and opaque beneath the skin.
Sometimes come dinnertime Sunday
I am still in my nightgown, the one
with the lace trim listing because
I have not mended it. Many days
I do not exercise, only
consider it, then rub my curdy
belly and lie down. Even
my poems are lazy. I use
syllabics instead of iambs,
prefer slant- to the gong of full rhyme,
write briefly while others go
for pages. And yesterday,
for example, I did not work at all!
I got in my car and I drove
to factory outlet stores, purchased
stockings and panties and socks
with my father's money.

To think, in childhood I missed only
one day of school per year. I went
to ballet class four days a week
at four-forty-five and on
Saturdays, beginning always
with plie, ending with curtsy.
To think, I knew only industry,
the industry of my race
and of immigrants, the radio
tuned always to the station
that said, Line up your summer
job months in advance. Work hard
and do not shame your family,
who worked hard to give you what you have.
There is no sin but sloth. Burn
to a wick and keep moving.

I avoided sleep for years,
up at night replaying
evening news stories about
nearby jailbreaks, fat people
who ate fried chicken and woke up
dead. In sleep I am looking
for poems in the shape of open
V's of birds flying in formation,
or open arms saying, I forgive you, all.

Affirmative Action Blues (1993)

Right now two black people sit in a jury room
in Southern California trying to persuade
nine white people that what they saw when four white
police officers brought batons back like
they were smashing a beautiful pinata was
"a violation of Rodney King's civil rights,"
just as I am trying to convince my boss not ever
to use the word "niggardly" in my presence again.
He's a bit embarrassed, then asks, but don't you know
the word's etymology? as if that makes it
somehow not the word, as if a word can't batter.
Never again for as long as you live, I tell him,
and righteously. Then I dream of a meeting
with my colleagues where I scream so loud the inside
of my skull bleeds, and my face erupts in scabs.
In the dream I use an office which is overrun
with mice, rats, and round-headed baby otters
who peer at me from exposed water pipes (and somehow
I know these otters are Negroes), and my boss says,
Be grateful, your office is bigger than anyone
else's, and maybe if you kept it clean you wouldn't
have those rats. And meanwhile, black people are dying,
beautiful black men my age, from AIDS. It was amazing
when I learned the root of "venereal disease"
was "Venus," that there was such a thing as a disease
of love. And meanwhile, poor Rodney King can't think
    straight;
what was knocked into his head was some addled notion
of love his own people make fun of, "Can we all

get along? Please?" You can't hit a lick with a crooked
stick; a straight stick made Rodney King believe he was
not a pinata, that amor vincit omnia.
I know I have been changed by love.
I know that love is not a political agenda, it lacks sustained
analysis, and we can't dance our way out of our
    constrictions.
I know that the word "niggardly" is "of obscure etymology"
    but probably derived from the French Norman, and that
    Chaucerand Milton and Shakespeare used it. It means
    "stingy," and the root is not the same as "nigger," which
    derives from"negar," meaning black, but they are
    perhaps, perhaps, etymologically related. The two "g"s
    are two teeth gnawing; rodent is from the Latin "rodere"
    which means "to gnaw," as I have said elsewhere.
I know so many things, including the people who love me
    and the people who do not.
In Tourette's syndrome you say the very thing that you are
    thinking, and then a word is real.
These are words I have heard in the last 24 hours which
    fascinate me: "vermin," "screed," "carmine," and
    "niggardly."
I am not a piñata, Rodney King insists. Now can't we all get
    along?

Haircut

I get off the IRT in front of the Schomburg Center for
Research in Black Culture after riding an early Amtrak from
Philly to get a hair cut at what used to be the Harlem "Y"
barbershop. It gets me in at ten to ten. Waiting, I eat fish
cakes at the Pam Pam and listen to the ladies call out orders:
bacon-biscuit twice, scrambled scrambled fried, over easy,
grits, country sausage on the side. Hugh is late. He sham-
poos me, says "I can't remember, Girlfriend, are you tender-
headed?" From the chair I notice the mural behind me in
the mirror. I know those overlapped sepia shadows, a
Renaissance rainforest, Aaron Douglas! Hugh tells me he
didn't use primer and the chlorine eats the colors every day.
He clips and combs and I tell him how my favorite Douglas
is called "Building More Stately Mansions," and he tells me
how fly I'd look in a Salt 'n' Pepa 'do, how he trained in
Japan.

Clip clip, clip clip. I imagine a whoosh each time my hair
lands on the floor and the noises of small brown mammals.
I remember, my father! He used to get his hair cut here,
learned to swim in the caustic water, played pool and
basketball. He cuts his own hair now. My grandfather
worked seventy-five years in Harlem building more stately
mansions. I was born two blocks away and then we moved.

None of that seems to relate to today. This is not my turf,
despite the other grandfather and great-aunt who sewed
hearts back into black chests after Saturday night stabbings

on this exact corner, the great-uncle who made a mosaic down the street, both grandmothers. What am I always listening for in Harlem? A voice that says, "This is your place, too," as faintly as the shadows in the mural? The accents are unfamiliar; all my New York kin are dead. I never knew Fats Waller but what do I do with knowing he used to play with a ham and a bottle of gin atop his piano; never went to Olivia's House of Beauty but I know Olivia, who lives in St. Thomas, now, and who exactly am I, anyway, finding myself in these ghostly, Douglas shadows while real ghosts walk around me, talk about my stuff in the subway, yell at me not to butt the line, beg me, beg me for my money?

What is black culture? I read the writing on the wall on the side of the "Y" as I always have: "Harlem Plays the Best Ball in the World." I look in the mirror and see my face in the mural with a new haircut. I am a New York girl; I am a New York woman; I am a flygirl with a new hair cut in New York City in a mural that is dying every day.

Judge Gets Grandma to Whip Offender

Instead of sending a drug offender to prison, a judge took off his belt and had the 18-year old defendant's grandmother whip the young man.

The defendant, Jamel Washington, needed "discipline, in the home and in the schools," the judge, Frank Eppes, said on Friday.

"I said, 'Grandmama, don't you think he needs a whipping?'" the judge said. "She said he needed one."

The whipping was conducted by the grandmother, 63-year old Victoria Washington Ellis.

For Miriam

Fields of iridescent, butter-lettuce green:
Germany a bright tail behind me
as I ride the train into Amsterdam's

impossible diphthongs, yellow or blue
"g"s stopping words in new places. Poets
travel and make poems about travel,

grasp at their travels as I do here.
"Land" was a word for "elsewhere" I used
in childhood, for storybook places where

other people lived. Italy: gondoliers
in tight, striped shirts, land of red and green noodles.
England: land of kings and queens, Elizabeth's

ermine-trimmed cape, her scepter and tiara,
Henry tearing at an outsized drumstick.
Germany: Adolph Hitler, mustachioed

Lucifer from another land, the Black
Forest where the Nazis had their revels,
my grandmother said. Now I have seen

Berlin's bullet-pocked buildings, the proud, scarred
church downtown, bolts of starry yellow fabric
stamped "JUDE" in black, train schedules and ledgers

a rage of numbers, a cemetery
of Saras. In a bombed-out lot at dusk, art
made of rubble rose from smoke and rap music.

I've drunk green, herb-tinted beer; eaten bags
of local cherries and light-brown bread;
been jostled in a market jazzed with

turmeric, pistachios, raw fish,
hemp and honey soaps, silver trinkets;
sweated in a hammam where Turkish women

dance naked for each other in the steam.
I know, this is hardly the sum of it.
In my Berlin dreams, Jesse Owens' legs

are a brown flurry speeding past the Fuhrer
in the name of another tribe, my own.
Here we talked about history, history,

history, which country forgets more, denies
more, and what is to be salvaged, in whose name?
Star-white jasmine, train-tracks without end —

This is what I have seen in your country, friend.

Sonnet

This morning I wished (once) to be a quiet
lover, but who can love with a closed mouth?
It opens, bites, is wet. The sounds come out.
Maybe it's how sounds release from corpses
when the undertaker turns them, last breath
sighing, free from will. In Mount Pleasant
I could hear elephants and tigers waking
each morning in the zoo, not copulating,
only trumpeting, roaring, announcing
their existence in indigenous tongues. These
noises I make are like dog whistles, air-raid
bells, touch-tones that tell the machine, play back
my messages, tell me who called, what they
said and who loves me, and why.

L.A. by Night

We're in a postcard, driving
down Hollywood Boulevard:
the car has fins, the palm trees
are pink, we wear cat-eye sun-
glasses in the L.A. night
glare, the neon chatter, blurred
white lights of speeding cars.
We are speed and light, flames
and fingers; all night
is a fistful of minutes,
a fast car, stars.

        Later,
we will make love loudly
in a room which belongs
to neither one of us, a room
strewn with our clothes and our
belongings. We will repeat
what we love most, our tongues
wise and specific. You'll say
I am a glow-worm, a cobalt star.

In L.A., the palm trees
are more ancient than they look
and objects closer than they
seem, but no city's myths
can explain our two moon faces
in the dark. We are zooming
and loud, fast hands, a bright
light, a magnificent
planet, L.A. by night.

Harlem Birthday Party

When my grandfather turned ninety we had a party
in a restaurant in Harlem called Copeland's.
Harlem restaurants are always dim to dark and this
was no exception. Daddy would have gone downtown
but Baba, as we called him, wanted to stay
in the neighborhood, and this place was "swanky."
We picked him up in his house on Hamilton Terrace.
His wife, "poor Minnette," had Alzheimer's disease
and thought Hordgie, who was not dead, was dead. She kept
cluck-clucking, "Poor Hordgie," and filling with tears.
They had organized a block watch on Hamilton
Terrace, which I was glad of; I worried always
about old people getting mugged; I was afraid
of getting old myself and knocked down in the street;
I was afraid it would happen to my grandfather.

My father moves fast always but in Harlem
something clicks into his walk which I love watching.
We fussed about taking a car, about parking;
in the end some walked, some drove, and the restaurant
parked the car for us. They treated my grandfather
like a Pope or like Duke Ellington. We ate salad,
fried chicken, mashed potatoes, broccoli, chocolate
cake, and Gustavo, who was then my boyfriend, cut
    Minnette's
meat for her and that became one of the things I would cite
forever when people asked me, how did you know
you wanted to marry him? I remember looking
at all the people at the party I had never seen,

and thinking, my grandfather has a whole life
we know nothing about, like at his funeral,
two years later, when a dreadlocked man about my age
went on and on about coming to Harlem
from Jamaica, they all said, talk to Mister Alex-
ander, and they talked, and my grandfather scolded,
advised, and today the young brother owns a patty stand.
in Brooklyn. Who ever knew this young man, or all the rest?

The star appearance at Copeland's, besides my father,
was my grandfather's wife's cousin, Jane Tillman Irving,
who broadcast on WCBS all-news radio.
What is a Harlem birthday party without a star?
What is a black family without someone
who's related to someone else who is a little
bit famous, if only to other black people?

And then goodbye, and then goodbye, and back
to New Haven, Washington, and Philadelphia,
where I lived with Gustavo. We walked downtown
after the party to Macy's to get feather pillows
on sale, and then we took Amtrak home. I cannot think
about this party without thinking how glad I am
we had it, that he lived long and healthy, that two years
later he was gone. He was born in Jamaica,
West Indies, and he died in Harlem, New York.

PART IV

Body of Life

1. 1990

One by one 'til
I'm the only one
left in the photo
we took in Gay Paree,
trill the final syl-
lable, thrill to
pretending we're
the Revue Negre,
funking so fiercely
our black clothes stained
our curvature, fab-
ulous flames let loose
in the city of lights.

One by one you leave
the picture, nix nix nix,
my moonpie face left
shining there. Au Revoir,
or like they say
in Sula, "'Vwah!", bright
as a bottle, the beau-
tiful children are
leaving me to trill
the final syllable,
this beautiful-
ugly world.

2. 1983

The other girls taught shy me to be a diva,
to preen, to plump my titties up like they did,

to work it. We danced. We wanted the body
of life and I lived for a year in that
body, the body of life, in D.C.,
in the African diaspora:
Chocolate City.

That was my slut year.
All the men I didn't sleep with, all I did,
all the lunch dates, all the dinners, all
the whistles on the streets of Chocolate
City, all the men who called me Baby,
called me Girl, like the one who made me tuna-
fish and tried to suck my breasts, then asked
me to type up his resume. My buzzer
in the middle of the night, my phone, a man
who greased me head to toe with Lubriderm,
a Cape Verdean who appeared on busses
and trains as if by divination, sketched
me naked, never spent the night. I told
one man how much I loved Betty Carter
and he said, I hope you're not one of those
bulldaggers. A lonely Nigerian
who cooked fufu and groped me on the sofa,
his across-the-ocean wife and daughter
watching from their picture frames.
Rum and dancing, too many things in my mouth,
genitals cobbled with passion or disease, bright
clitoris a phantom limb, remembering –

I moved away to Boston and would call
you for the update: Renee was a samba
star at Brasil Tropical, shimmied
on Brazilian TV. Denise graduated
school and made the foreign service, moved
to Jamaica, to a bungalow, with
a man and a maid named Pansy. "Who's sick?"

I'd ask and you'd tell me, and who died,
and one day you said, "And I'm living with AIDS."

There was Kemron in Kenya.
You were saving to get it.
You met with a support group
of other black men. You had
a Dominican boyfriend,
same as me. Mostly you felt
O.K., but you hated
your medicine. You were fat,
but you still took class.
No, Tyrone wasn't sick. But David was dead.

It was Njambi who called me to say,
you were back in shape. You performed
for the visiting Eminence of Senegal,
the next day went into the hospital,
the next day died. It made a romantic
story, but you're still gone. "I love when you call me
because you're alive," you said once,
one of your few friends still alive.
I'm writing this poem to say how we were,
that we danced and fucked and sweated, loved
ourselves and each other, lived fiercely,
knew joy. I'm writing to say,
I got lucky, you were my friend, you
knew me as a girl, I am a woman,
now, with my little piece of your story,
the year of the body of life.

3. 1994

(In my neighborhood now I watch women who are lovely
at a distance and lurid up close cross the street serving much
runway, much attitude, and I am Ovaltine, a walrus, no
longer sharp and spangled. In my half-sleep I hear teeth
sucking from the dead, the divas awakening to coach me:
Never let on you are less than fabulous, one says, hissing
in disgust at all the home-training I've forgotten, so I pull
myself together and whistle, a bald, brown, and beautiful
Yul Brynner singing Deborah Kerr's lines: Whenever I feel
afraid, I hold my head erect, and whistle a happy tune, so
no one will suspect I'm afraid.

Life is only momentarily fearless; life is only for a moment
full of cures; the body, as always, tells the round, bald truth
when my stomach grips to say, no cure in sight.)

Dream #3

I wake from the dream another person, tasting metal or salt,
smelling turpentine, my shoulder askew and my jaw out of
whack. My father has not been stabbed in the hip by the
auto mechanic, stabbed impossibly with a blunt hammer. I
do not have to decide, do I call, do I not call the cops, what
would Daddy want, or do; Oh God. None of this was real,
but I know that strange things happen, that I dreamed to call
my grandfather just before he died to find out his parents'
names, and I did, and he died, and no one had known they
were Emma and James, so even though now I can wash my
face, eat lunch, and feel secure that Daddy is not dying
on the lawn in Connecticut, that I was not raped even
though I can smell the mechanic's rancid hair as I struggle to
perceive my real body while symbols float around me in a
rain of draughtsman's cut-outs: telephone, hammer, oil can,
mechanic, I still wonder why I dreamed it, how I dreamed it,
how is Daddy, how am I.

Dream

You come back from the evil where you've been so long
living and dying in a crusty, tired voice,
come back to hold me and tell me goodbye
in the Daskalides voice I first knew, and loved.
You take me to your bed and are suddenly naked,
and plump. You leave your glasses on. Your curls come back.
Then your best friend comes into the bed, who is my friend,
too, who is not yet sick but will be, and we lie
together, all of us naked and beautiful.
I smell your shit faintly, like a lover's known smells
toward the end of the day, like we know and love
and smell New York City – your penis bleeds a little
and your best friend licks it healed.

                                 This is where it all
began: with love and ecstasy. I cry watching
these two men, the first tears because of it
since three years ago in a hotel lobby when
you told me everyone, everyone we knew
who was going to die of this. It was like
the awful first truth of childhood: yes, Mama will
die one day, but not for a long time, yes Daddy,
and dying is real, yes, you. That was when I used to dream
my family on the chain gang, in the desert, gone.
That was when I used to dream myself in a party dress
buckled to a chair inside a huge machine
which churned out shit. This is a new dream. I am grown.

We three are talking about poems, about Robert

Hayden's Coke-bottle glasses, about how the only time
he wrote of love it was lonely and austere.
Love is a dream where someone is dying, the faint
smell of shit and the memory of poems that breathe
for us each in this bed. I kiss you on the mouth
and I am crying, not just dreaming, not quite
certain, like when I would dream myself on the toilet
reading "Hagar the Horrible" and wake up
having peed the bed: The Wet Bed Dream.
    The clock reads
seven-eleven. This I know because I opened
up my eyes, because I can.

Blues

Wrigley illuminates
the night sky violet,

indigo city tonight,
Chicago, city

surrounded by Magikist lips,
baci baci baci

benedicting the expressways.
"Sixty-watt gloom" suffused

Hayden's Detroit, the South
Side's similar neon face.

I elegize cities
and leave them, cities

my imagined Atlantises.
Tonight, all Chicago

is singing the blues.
Autumn came today,

winter next, always.
Elegy, indigo, blues.

Equinox

Now is the time of year when bees are wild
and eccentric. They fly fast and in cramped
loop-de-loops, dive-bomb clusters of conversants
in the bright, late-September out-of-doors.
I have found their dried husks in my clothes.

They are dervishes because they are dying,
one last sting, a warm place to squeeze
a drop of venom or of honey.
After the stroke we thought would be her last
my grandmother came back, reared back and slapped

a nurse across the face. Then she stood up,
walked outside, and lay down in the snow.
Two years later there is no other way
to say, we are waiting. She is silent, light
as an empty hive, and she is breathing.

At the Beach

Looking at the photograph is somehow not
unbearable: My friends, two dead, one low
on T-cells, his white T-shirt an X-ray
screen for the virus, which I imagine
as a single, swimming paisley, a sardine
with serrated fins and a neon spine.

I'm on a train, thinking about my friends
and watching two women talk in sign language.
I feel the energy and heft their talk
generates, the weight of their words in the air
the same heft as your presence in this picture,
boys, the volume of late summer air at the beach.

Did you tea-dance that day? Write poems
in the sunlight? Vamp with strangers? There is
sun under your skin like the gold Sula
found beneath Ajax's black. I calibrate
the weight of your beautiful bones, the weight
of your elbow, Melvin,

                    on Darrell's brown shoulder.

Cleaning Out Your Apartment

A fifty-year-old resume
that says you raised delphiniums.
Health Through Vegetable Juice,
your book of common prayer,

your bureau, bed, your easy chair,
dry Chivas bottles, mop and broom,
pajamas on the drying rack,
your shoe trees, shoe-shine box.

I keep your wicker sewing kit,
your balsa cufflink box. There's
only my framed photograph to say,
you were my grandfather.

Outside, flowers everywhere,
the bus stop, santeria shop.
Red and blue, violent lavender.
Impatiens, impermanent, swarm.

Tending

In the pull-out bed with my brother
    in my grandfather's Riverton apartment
my knees and ankles throbbed from growing,
    pulsing so hard they kept me awake –
or was it the Metro North train cars
    flying past the apartment, rocking the walls,
or was it the sound of apartment front doors
    as heavy as prison doors clanging shut?
Was the Black Nation whispering to me
    from the Jet magazines stacked on the floor, or
was it my brother's unfamiliar ions
    vibrating, humming in his easeful sleep?
Tomorrow, as always, Grandfather will rise
    to the Spanish-Town cock's crow deep in his head
and perform his usual ablutions,
    and prepare the apartment for the day,
and peel fruit for us, and prepare a hot meal
    that can take us anywhere, and onward.
Did sleep elude me because I could feel
    the heft of unuttered love in his tending
our small bodies, love a silent, mammoth thing
    that overwhelmed me, that kept me awake
as my growing bones did, growing larger
    than anything else I would know?

Leaving

Presence and absence are too absolute
to describe the way you were those last years,
Nana, always there in varying degrees.
One day you sat up and asked about "Doctor
Du Bois's great book" and you were not confused.
In one of your long quiet stretches I dreamed
you were on the cover of Parade magazine
in a yellow tunic and yellow leggings
(yes, I know, you never wore yellow)
sitting cross-legged in a field, telling
your secrets of aging well.

                When you died
we gathered and wept over your body
and stroked your beautiful hair. You're not buried
anywhere, so there's no metaphor to visit.
You told me when I was too young to hear
that you wanted to donate your body
to science, Howard University
Medical School, and then cremation.
The urn is too literal, and anyway,
I don't know where Mom put it. You visit me
still in my dreams, full-blown for moments
then elsewhere   goodbye   and that's
the way it is, now, that's the way it is.

After

It wasn't as deep as I expected,
your grave, next to the grandmother who died
when I was three. I threw a flower in
and fizzled off the scene like carbonation.
My body of course remained but all else
was a cluster of tiny white bubbles
floating up, up, up, to an unseen top.

I wore your vicuna coat and an ill-
fitting cloche from Alexanders. I walked
among the rows, away from the men
covering the coffin, which was when I saw
"X," Malcolm, a few yards down, "Paul Robeson,"
then "Judy Garland" then – the car was waiting
and we had to go.

       The cocktail parties
must be something there! You'd discuss self-help
and the relative merits of Garvey-
ism with Malcolm. Robeson would read
in a corner. Judy, divine in black
clam-diggers, would throw back her head
and guffaw, smoke as many cigarettes
as she wanted.

Before you died I dreamed
of cocktail parties in your Harlem
apartment where you'd bring all our dead kin
back to life, for me! I was old enough
to drink with you, to wear a cocktail dress.
Like the best movies, the dream was black
and white, except for my grandmother's
lipstick, which was red.